Here, There and Nowhere
Valery Oisteanu
with collages by Ruth Oisteanu

SPUYTEN DUYVIL

New York City

Cover Art and illustration collages: Ruth Oisteanu
Editors: Allen Sheinman, Ruth Oisteanu
Text technical support: Robert Heiger
Cover graphics: Robert Heiger
Author's photo: Daniel Root

Library of Congress Control Number: 2024933118

for my wife
on our
50th wedding anniversary

Poetry books written in English by Valery Oisteanu

Underground Shadows (Pass Press, New York, 1977)

Underwater Temples (Pass Press, New York, 1979)

Do Not Defuse (Pass Press, New York, 1980)

Vis-a-vis Bali (New Observation Press, New York, 1985)

Passport to Eternal Life (Pass Press, New York, 1990)

Moons of Venus (Pass Press, New York, 1992)

Temporary Immortality (Pass Press, New York, 1995)

ZEN DADA (Linear Art Press, New York, 1999)

Perks in Purgatory (Fly by Night Press, New York, 2009)

Anarchy for a Rainy Day (Spuyten Duyvil, New York, 2015)

Lighter Than Air (Spuyten Duyvil, New York, 2017)

In the Blink of a Third Eye (Spuyten Duyvil, New York, 2020)

Forward

Welcome to a work of poetry documenting my own and my wife Ruth's surreal experiences traveling the world, from the U.S. to Mexico, Romania, Italy and beyond. My poems are spontaneous recollections of traumatic events, fragments of forgotten dreams, nebulous states of mind, illogical episodes and subliminal sequences of ecstasy and redemption. Some are imbued with anguish and a restless longing for resolution.

In a way, these poems are collages of words snatched from out-of-body experiences that conjure visions from a surreal universe made personal, marked by uncontainable desire or an implosion of vulnerability. The pictorial collages refer to Ruth's personal experiences derived from dreams and nightmares gotten from our travels.

V. O.

TABLE OF CONTENTS

I.
The Mexican Notebook

WE MARCH

We march and we march some more
We march at dawn and we march at daybreak
We march with our twisted feet and tired hands
Past the police huddled in their trucks
And the national guard huddled with guns
We march for the end of wars and for better human rights
We march in the polluted streets and demand clean water
Past the multibillionaire palaces protected by the army
And we march for the women trafficked abroad
And for workers dying at work
We march in our sleep
We march all night
We march 'til we die.

LANDSCAPE OF AN UNFINISHED DREAM

This is a poem inside a poem
A sax player below my balcony at Casa de Adobe
Goats and chickens roam across the street
An oasis in the middle of favela shacks
Light enters through a broken stone in the wall
A huge wooden double door that goes nowhere
Down the street in a sub-basement there are some poets
They speak to me between curtains, no faces, only voices
Leaning on a bicycle that collapses, causing a domino effect
As one bike falls on top of another
No dream ends well despite a series of yellow-red murals
Large faces of women create a cinematic effect
Aqua Potable flashes on the side of a truck
Chili peppers dry in a mortar and pestle
Add green tomatoes and steaming tamales
Spicy mescal and more mouth-burning food
Father appears briefly; he's not a drinker
But nevertheless he is very drunk
Walking away into the mountains of Monte Alban
Where trees are blooming with white flowers
Just stones, ancient stones, miles and miles
Jaguars, bats, snakes carved into the palaces
It's stifling hot even in the shade
Running down into the land of the Virgin of Solitude
Into the land of 3,000 churches
What have they done? Oh God! It's too late
Too late to wake up
The dream inside the dream goes on.

La Punta

Nightspot in Puerto Escondido, Oaxaca, Mexico

The sounds of hallucinatory guitars and drums drown the sidewalk
It's a zoo of tattooed eyelids and face masks
"Puta!" scream the Colombian hooligans
An Amy Winehouse lookalike belts out "Valery"
Frida's Paradise Alley bar and restaurant vibrates
Argentinians devour industrial-size guacamole dishes
Washing them down with Mescal, we are in Oaxaca
The land of agave cacti and hidden poverty
Here smoke and margaritas roll and vape
Under a full moon moaning
Nights of unextinguished chaos
A fever of hormones, a fever of motorcycle exhaust
Exaltation, expurgation and ejaculation
Desire burnt out prematurely in cheap hotels
Hashish pipes empty at last
The everlasting craving for adventure
Evaporates over the rough Pacific Ocean.

Oaxacan Shrooms

Projections appear in the white sky
The dead artists are staring at me
Frida Kahlo, Tamayo, Alvarez Bravo
Hairless dogs chase me mercilessly
No rest for the weary poet
Dark streets, bicycle taxis, an injured right leg
The turtle dove sits on the terrace table
So many cacti blocking the passage of time
Mescal in a bottle, in a medicinal jar
The pyramids majestically calling
Toward the direction of the moon and the sun
The confluence of Venus and Mercury
Teotihuacan, abandoned city, lost civilization
The ghosts of Artaud, Kerouac, Carrington, Varo and Rahon
Tarahumaras gathering in a peyote circle
Flying trance images of serpentine fire
Feathered god, jade leopard, lapis lazuli eye
Clay dancers breaking into pieces
Mexico mon amour punishing journey
Drumbeats echoing within my chimeras
Black Urakas birds awaken me from the nightmare
A huge army of long-legged insects
Arranged as a poem by Octavio Paz
A map of hidden water among the stones.

Across the Cathedral in Oaxaca

A skeleton rides a bike
Makes the sign of the cross
Children sing "La Cucaracha"
A man carries a naked mannequin:
A woman with the head of a crocodile
The short village ladies sell scarfs
While a blind man plays the harmonium
2,000 churches of the Virgin Mary
Of Guadeloupe, of Soledad, of Oaxaca
The Tamayo Museum suffers a worker's strike
A mole in all the food, pyramids snaking up the mountain
Advertisements for Monte Alban private tours
16th-century bathrooms for posterity
Give us Holy Guacamole our daily food
Some classic music next to a salsa joint
Our Mescal-tasting tour ends in a restaurant
Where are my friends, the poets and painters?
Where are the surrealists of Mexico?

BRIZAS DE ZICATELA

Waves biting the shores, the rocks and the sand
Next to palm trees, boats fish for lobsters feeding tourists,
The ginger flowers blush with a red sadness
That bleed into candles like open wounds
Skydivers jump from small planes
Scarring the sky with their parachutes
A young girl with an Afro drowns by the shore
The undertow is merciless and no one seems to care
No lifeguards to be seen, sleeping on their lunch break
People are busy with Christmas decorations
A huge tree lights up the beach in Zicatela
Next to it an ice cream vendor runs out of ice cream
He scrapes the last scoop of strawberry for a small boy
Children are playing with fake boxes, empty of presents
Sand buggies leave behind a smell of exhaust and gasoline
Paradise is just a state of mind
This hotel is for sale
This happiness is too expensive
This sleep story is fractured, no more cakes
No reservations, no sitting
Carbon monoxide a big headache
Keep flapping your wings faster and faster
A car siren announces the first day of winter
the solstice is upon us, nothing can stop it
It's 85 degrees and the lone white gull
Falls silently from his endless journey.

BIO-LUMINESCENT LAGOON

Escaping down 24 steps at the Santa Fe Hotel
Where iguanas are reclaiming their territory
Falcons chasing the pigeons, newly hatched from eggs
A quiet ghost makes the nightlight flicker
As a blackout continues for several hours
It's time for the Hanukah hag Sameha candles
Time to jump into the bioluminescent lagoon
Whose glowing green waters are stirred up by boats
Where plankton radiate and cling to the skin
Jumping into the dark waters of Puerto Escondido
Frightened, wearing an orange life preserver
Crocodiles hate ugly plastic vests
So a quick dunk and back into the boat
All aglow with plankton, glimmering in the waves
At last, a return to civilization
Where mescal flows freely
Mixing with the crashing of Pacific Ocean waves.

THE BLACK EGGS OF TEOTIHUACAN

Quetzalcoatl, the plumed serpent, flies over enigmatic ruins
Down the Avenue of the Dead, destroyed by their own
People who worshiped Venus and Mercury
A secret tunnel runs below the Sun pyramid
As the Moon temple reaches toward the sky
Many underground passages lined with jade statues
A giant jaguar fresco covers a buried wall
Every entrance an enigma, each exit a mystery
The rain god Tlaloc brews the elixir of agave-mescal
Mixing with lye it becomes glue for the stones
Lapis lazuli grinded become paints for sky and water
Where are the Olmecs, the Toltecs, the Zapotecs
The indigenous people of Teotihuacan?
Seven major civilization lost in Pre-Colombian Mezzoamerica
20,000 years ago humans walked the Valley of Mexico
Watching the sky and astronomical events
They radiated a new culture that entered my soul
And intoxicated my brain.

The Landscape of Sleep Deprivation

Strange sounds over the night sky of Oaxaca,
Fireworks explosion with no lightnings or colors.
Birds are chatting from the palm trees,
Workers are grinding the stones of a new swimming pool,
Motorcycles zooming by, jumping over speed bumps.
A jet carrying more tourists crossing the clouds
A stone waterfall creaks in the distance
Street food vendors are cooking with weird smells
No rest for the weary poet
Every café has a guitar player
Street musicians packing their gear after a long session
An assemblage of tap dancers and saxophone players
Overload of vendors hocking carpets
Barking sidewalks, shouting graffities
One says "military assassin" on the walls of a school building
Orderly marching soldiers bring down the Mexican flag
It's never quiet in Oaxaca
Day or dark
Exhausted listening to the cacophony of despair.

Dolphins Are Jumping for Free

We chase black birds in the morning
We avoid the iguanas in the afternoon
The pigeons cooing all through the day
Ants invading the room through the front door
There is no quiet place in Puerto Escondido
Day Market, Night Market
Young men hocking souvenirs under a scorching sun
Buy the hammock, buy the necklaces
Spend your pesos 'til the end
The ATM machines are out of order
But for sure you have dollars or a credit card
We'll take it. Just purchase anything
A glowing T-shirt with a psychedelic jaguar
A hat with a gecko patch
A bag of organic coffee
A wooden spoon
A ceramic turtle
A bottle of mescal
No bargaining
It's all under Sinaloa Cartel control
A fixed price for a massage or a hand-woven outfit
Only the dolphins are still jumping for free.

DREAMSCAPE II

Cows on stilts cross the flood waters
Shepherds, in ethnic robes, also on stilts
Policemen puzzled by this action
Squint in a fog of a strange mists
All is flooded and covered with milky waters
The scenery interrupted by cracks in the landscape
As far as one can see
X marks the spot where strange rituals took place
Who built this house full of people looking like rag dolls
With expressions of surprise on their faces?
Rooms and rooms of white plaster walls
Crashing waves waking me in the middle of the night
As a bird crashes through the fragile window
The shower door comes crashing down, shattering panels
Water drips from the sockets
An explosion of fireworks next to catapulting bottles
It's never quiet in this endless reverie
Mama pigeons hatching their naked babies
14 images of Frida Khalo crowd the jewelry store
Frightened voices of surfers and paragliders seep through the cracks
In the tattoo dormitory, it's movie night
Hunger games in see-through underwear
Stars tattooed on bronze asses
A Mexican comida at Café Chino, hot and spicy
Hit the Road, Jack Kerouac!
Your Mexico City Blues resonate in La Punta
A revolver band sings by the pool in Frida's paradise
It's the second day of Hanukkah
And there is no pot in my latkes
Please put pot in my latkes!

II.
Ukrainian Songs

Sunflowers of Bucha

The sun is bursting with gunfire across Ukraine
Looking at Stash's photos from the front line
Huge yellow flowers blossom on abandoned tanks
Growing over and under the rusting trucks
Graffiti painted by the weakened survivors
The sky is scarred by rockets shrieking above
As dead soldiers lie in the mud, in the streets
Sunflowers stretch their yellow petals upward
Through rusted armored vehicles riddled with bullets
While the flowers bleed over murdered Ukrainians
They bleed in cold dark basements
In the frigid bombed churches of Irpim
Burning candles warm their fingers
Readying to strike across the Dnipro
Orphaned children wander without light or bread
Painting sunflowers on war carcasses
While the invader's ghosts scurry away
Drowning in pools of dirty black water
There will be no peace until liberation
Otherwise those heroes died for nothing.

THE DARK SUN OF WAR

The rain falls over the ruins of Bahmut
Tanks, painted with a "Z," burn in the fields
Silence is a luxury during these battles
Where every artillery shell equals a casualty
Yesterday's hardened criminals become today's dead heroes
Until the Gulag Archipelago of prisons is depleted
But the bloody rain still descends from sunrise to sunset
Trucks with young men slowly rumble
To kill, to rape, to loot, to kidnap children
While only coffins come back from the front
Time to wake up, underground comrades
From Belarus to Kazakhstan to Crimea
Stand up to nuclear rattling, no nukes in Belarus
Sacrifice war ideology and Putin's promises
Let's speak peace, Slavic brothers, now
Before we become inhuman, demolishing
The ancient history of common Christianity
The rain will not wash away all the blood spilled
The sky remains fire-red and dark in the Ukraine
One candle burns in a broken window
Damn the war, sing praises for the heroes
A eulogy for peace on the edge of mass graves
As the raindrops beat the drums of WWIII
Maybe it's already here, only the rain knows.

Liuba

Liuba lost her lover in the war
She lost her future in a split second
The memory of a bleeding gun
The scope scarred, the glass shattered
Liuba is cooking potatoes and beans
In the trenches, salting them with her tears
To a young recruit: Have a plate of food
You are about to lose your virginity
As mortars fall, speeding up his heartbeat
He buries his face in her thighs
Vlodimir never had a woman like that
She then offers herself to the next sniper
No Virgin left behind,
The unit will survive as a man.

THE LONGEST NIGHT

An agitated ocean pushes angry waves, snapping surfboards
On Playa Zicatela salty waters crest at 90 feet
Meandering footprints end at the water's edge
At Café Olvidada, La Bruja, the smell of burnt coffee
The longest night is not over quite so soon
Moans of an earth beaten and battered by climate
Scarred by volcanoes, wrinkled by earthquakes
Polluted by oil-spills and military missions
Sleep no more, the night will be gone as darkness prevails
Skeletons crawl across booby-trapped Ukrainian plains
Soon the sun will burn through the wounds
Scars will map out the journey of survival
From the Black Sea to the borders of Poland
No sleep for the dictator on the Stealth Train
The longest night of the cruelest war
The sun peaks, hallucinatory, through palm trees
Breaking suddenly into a victorious day.

THE PEACE ENIGMA OF STILLNESS

Herds of trees stumble in the distance
Wailing below a dark undertow
Some fall toward the empty sky
Burning with the speed of an invasion
How hard they try to become birds
A flock of trees experience death
Flying below their immortality horizon
Nothing is left behind but timelessness
The sky undresses for the sunrise
As laughter disappears beneath frozen waterfalls
This is the startling winter landscape of WWIII
A shark's smile tattooed onto toys of war
Thousands of blacksmiths forging new death tools
Others assembling coffins with no names
For the unmarked crosses of the young
Dressed in white, little green men
Sad prisoners of vodka and greed
Like termites swarming European plains
Fashioned into coal-dust body bags
Screams of scars and excrement cover the snow
Oh mother of death, they do not have to perish
Lips of an icy corpse will never drink the wine
This blood-drenched earth was once a forest
In the depth of winter persists an invincible summer.

The Revolutionary Cultural Exchange

Through the fog of tear gas and pepper spray
Resistance tools bloom like wild flowers
Against brutal police military aggression
Around the world, from Hong Kong to Portland
From Santiago to Nantes, from Washington to Beirut
Orange traffic cones are topped with reversed
Water bottles against tear-gas canisters
Place the cone on top of the can, squeeze the bottle, kill the gas!
The tennis racket volleys with a backhand to the cylinder
And back at the aggressors black-helmeted heads
They bark, we sing, they attack, we stay unmoved
The audacity of defiance unchained
Living in a police state with excessive intimidation
A simple umbrella is a flower of defense in Ferguson
Hiding the faces of peaceful protesters from facial recognition
Leaf-blowers dispersing outlawed gas and suffocating smells
The flowers of resistance against autocracy grow globally
In Greece, in Catalonia, in Mexico, in Wisconsin
Blasting the surveillance camera with laser pointers, with black spray paint
The powers of imagination are arrayed against
Prohibition and full-gear paternalism
Manipulation of behavior, restricted freedom of speech give a certitude of power
Water cannons and tanks against cyclists will never work
Struggle is a state of mind, awakened consciousness
Defend your rights, resist, persist, walk to the edge of life and death
The military invaders will hang themselves with tools of suppression
Freedom continues to grow in the harshest terrain
As clenched fists and open brave hearts march on.

Navalny Blues

In a narrow cell padded with silence
On the gulag corridors to Purgatory
Walks the last hope for Russia without Putin
The cruel wind whistles through the cracks
Kafka trials stretch sentences beyond life
Cannibalistic theater of extreme cruelty
The evil clouds cover the Russian sky
The only hope is a true revolution
But no one has time for it
No one showed up for the protest march
Where is the underground press?
Where are the Sakharovs of today?
All poisoned, killed, caged, afraid
Brainwashed by nationalistic neo-fascism
Generations obliterated of free will.
Submissive heartless torturers, empty
Of impossible dreams of a country
Without FSB, without war and oligarchs
Storm the gates of the prisons and liberate
Navalny, Kara-Muzra and all political prisoners
There will be no happiness in Russia
No laughter…only Navalny blues

III.
The Gotham Blues

DRIVING IN MANHATTAN

The East Village wakes up with the usual noise,
an urban landscape born of the mother
of permanent construction,
tinting the avenues with orange stripes.

Streets and roads are under a perpetual holy reconstruction.
Orange cone armies are strategically artranged to
choke the traffic;
orange barrels block every road.

The roads to hell are paved with cones,
psychedelic witch hats protruding from the underground,
a symphony of syncopation controlling
via orange cymbals.

Slow down. Do not turn.
Do not go anywhere.
The flowers of evil blossom
on the Avenue of the Americas.

No Title Needed

Welcome to the end of the mind,
where rocks turn into dust,
branches into mulch,
waterfalls into mud and muck
with the smell of exhaustion.
Here where the caves of ancestral ghosts
multiply shadows,
birds feed on other birds
sleepwalking over shimmering paths,
over treetops, over cupolas
and mysterious rooftops.
No place to hide, no place to run,
no place to die.
Somebody clarifies the notion of loneliness
unfenced, untalkative, unnoticed… terminal.

PRIMITIVE MEANINGLESS BLUES

Gazing at the cold, quaking landscape
The moon peeks through a hole in a cloud
And then through a crack in a wall
Over a cemetery of soiled washing machines
Smelling of a mannequin's toenails and fresh-cut hair
Verses, not needing sleep, burst from memory
At midnight a cake with a blue wig appears on a sidewalk
A hairy-eyed clock disguised by strong vapors of ether
Strikes the cords of a shattered movement
Too exhausted to radiate sardonic smells
Human-scented, pigeon-stained, extract of nothingness
Barefoot, riding a stolen bike and absolved of any guilt
Eardrums pierced by constant demolition
The sky is broken at the elbow, a clash of flashes
Stained by red birds, invisible against the dark
Volcanos erupting orange metal vomit
Fusing all the dead whales in a broken habitat
Do not step on the poet escaping the shell-scented jungle
The unconscious desires, the uncontrollable nightmare
All discreetly sealed in an underwater underworld
Escaping the dying desert of forgotten dreams.

CITYSCAPE BY NIGHT

A full moon climbs the stone walls of a chapel
Below a Manhattan that never sleeps
In the sky tiny eggs collide and drip down
Into a movie set of Little Italy in action
As an angry mafia boss escapes from a building
While a motorcycle gang rolls across the avenue
A samurai sword accompanies broken beer bottles
Cutting through the darkness of unmarked alleys
A man lies, bleeds on the cobblestone pavement
Ninjas run beside us down the polluted street
There is a vast emptiness in this chaos
An abandoned shoe, an orphan glove, a half-eaten apple
Smells of fish crawl out of dark shuttered markets
The huge nothingness of old sneakers hanging in pairs
From phone wires above dusty windows
Only the moon-bow rises through the clouds
Shining like a mandala of the Terra Incognita Magnetica.

GOTHAM CITY TOUR GUIDE

American Indian women watch in disbelief
A sleepless Purgatory waiting to be loved
Flying tailors take measurements
East Village-style with pierogis on the side
Angels of Pepsi Cola lie asleep in buzzing chains
As the death of a pierced nipple rusts inside a saxophone
The Ramones' three-legged cat sleeps at CBGB
Wiring people, tagging, tracking society
Cleansing our brain with a new religion
Invisible Underwater Umbrellas Club members
Drip blood over a graffiti of fingernails
Loudly singing from the broken windows
Of an abandoned rainy building
At our Disassociation Meetings every Tuesday
The Boredom Club of Laughing Dentists
Is an isolation station for grieving families
Navigating aborted routes to nowhere
Anticipation blues spin the web
Bones rattle the music of Gotham
Chaotic matter fills the forest of metal
Our kinetic city changes the allegory of wisdom.

ASSISTED REVOLUTION
(IN CENTRAL PARK)

Faces of granite sculptures, in transitory loneliness
Sad interlocked trees hanging over benches
Flowers disturbing the textures of footprints and hoof marks
A long-haul chess man receives a call of apprehensive spring

Pandemic masks, toxic outfits of doom
Mask robbers unite, the future is yours
Vaccinated three times and a booster
Face-shielded anonymous heads and plague shoes

Revolutionize post-pandemic sex desires
Effortlessly flowing through the bridges of eyes
Stuffed horses pull carriages sheepishly
While bikers run consecutively along the Central Park path

There is no melody in the string of noises
It is a sad afternoon of wounded lost souls
Melting daylight, chained for all eternally to water
Birds chat of savage mad love by the fountain
Small boats and ducks lost in the wind
Compete in arousing colors under sunlight
It's a touch of grace in the sounds of bird talk
On the other side of the space-time continuum.

THE SUBWAY IN THE SKY

Daydreaming in the afternoon, waking on the uptown local
I go up to the street, where the tablecloth of air unfolds
Colored shades of blue, between emaciated buildings
Smothered in red, swaying rhythmically from left to deep left
A cruise ship moored on the rocks, drops cripping humans
Water cascades out of churches, revealing tiled swans
Pain killed in play, sardonic nostrils of the eardrums vibrate
To the accelerated staccato of the frolicking Betty Boop
Crashed birds land in the assigned tragedy of a three-headed snake
Vertical balconies of destiny are stacked beyond the clouds
Guitar riffs encircle the Lychee gardens
Sunken enigmas glide, anguished dreams in slanted skyscrapers
Angular crystal decanters house red cardinals
A cluttered subway car passes without a motorman
Driving us all past the repetitious destinations
Next stop: shamanic desperado amnesia
At the side of the rivers in silent confluence
Where transient sadness is barely recognized
and exchanged for ephemeral erotic insanity
possessed in a city that is not even there.

So It Seems

(APPROPRIATELY DEPRESSING)

Poem half remembered from an illusion
Wrinkled like aging female breasts
Getting smaller, flattened under my feet
Lost among the living and the dead

Spreading the solitude of shattered sleep
Expanding psychedelically without meaning
The moon rises under my night tongue
Grinding the galaxies, planets and stars

Leaving the eloquence of the soul behind
An insanity forecast of the hermetically sealed Ego
Believing in images melted away, lost
Surviving the cemetery where there is no exit

Metallic noises under the Manhattan bridge
And a sliver of Earth: East River Park
Smiling at the cement jungle of Brooklyn and Queens
Where noise echoes with humanoid charm

Waiting for post-Covid Godot
In the ridiculous disappearing caldron
In the labyrinths of the Lower East River
While above, flying cacti smile wolfishly.

My Wife Ruth

Her breasts move counter-clockwise to each other
Her eyes never sleep in dreams and beyond
A witness to her parents' tragedy and redemption
A quiet teacher of Holocaust studies
A bead alchemist, her wrists covered in bracelets
Zena the fortune teller with henna tats
A bridge partner till the bitter end
A tongue of simultaneous critique and praise
Collage-master with a surreal magic twist
Gardener of exotic plants outdoors, indoors
Her hands create the secret greenhouse
Her songs make the flowers sway and shiver
As chandeliers dance and cling to the salsa beat
A fountain of silver rings slung over her shoulder
Swaying and dodging the dangling wares
Watching melting watches cling to the piano.

SOMETHING MELTING IN MY EYE

No more sleeping on the roof of imagination
A repurposed volcano exhales smoke and fireballs
The scent of burnt onyx and fresh lava
The velocity of birds stronger than crystallization
Perforating my senses, drilling the clouds
There, where the red-eyed time traveler begins all over again
Eat my brain — the interior of the inside
Where a cluster of musical notes dies on a sheet of paper
Shaking like a leaf in the autumn sky
Something is thawing in my eye
The extract of nothingness
The last branch of a golden poplar
Close my eyelid and breath deep
The fiery tongue spits poetry
No matter how long the scream
A net of neurons protrude and bend my mind
For all the women that I have loved
Maybe it was just a dream that ended before I woke up.

IV.
Woodstock Snapshots

THE FOREST SHAMANISTA

Let me be your wabi-sabi guide of the forest
With sequential blinking lights at the entrance
Psychedelic melting colors snaking backward
As perching wild turkeys carpet-bomb visitors
Assisted by squirrels' precision blasting of nuts
Birds continue to bark with intraspecies sounds
Coyotes howl and wild cats menace behind trees
My Third Eye travels over and under bear trails
Watching them training cubs to break into parked cars
Lepidoptera and infinite insects converge quickly
While only the bees know the secret coves of honeycombs
Birds of the dead waterfalls nest in driftwood decay
The imperfect tarnished landscape unfolds bewildered
Into a withered orchestra of dry logs and branches
Tree trunks sprouting horizontal dried fish
Listen to my whistle, hear my healing drumbeat
Follow the path into my sacred cave labyrinth
Each handprint is a petroglyph of spider webs
Observe the mystical initiation begin to unfold.

CAPTIVE CATSKILL LANDSCAPE

A mysterious wingless wind hides in the hammock
Covering his scaly snake body with crimson leaves
Howling by the melancholic doors, by the windows
The scent of mountain lions, bears and deer creep in
Where old withered flowers strip themselves of petals
Soon the fallen branches will become firewood
A weightless sky bares its teeth, gusts lift the flower pots
Putrefied brown leaves take over the musty alleys
Cylindrical disembodied tree trunks in a chaotic circle
The wind bomb hauls up shrubs and dead layers of soil
Rustling, hissing, crashing, blowing, shrieking
Chasing wailing wild boars and pine cones
Too late to reverse migratory geese that refuse
To come back toward the dead eye of the moon
Surrounded by mountains and twisted tree limbs
The forest fluttering in its cold damp dream
Shrouded, scorched with ghastly pungency
Strangely clouded, incessantly burning
Somber apocalyptic, pestilential captive fires
Blacken the corners of this unfathomable season.

WOODSTOCK RAIN

It's still August, and my poems are broken in half
Shattered stanzas, wrecked words, broken beats
Random sounds of crashing branches and squirrels' nuts
Trees tumbling into the creek, the dark waters
Flowing trembling into the tributary
The dispirited birds are barely singing
It's about to rain, boringly, without hope
Calm before the summer shower
Dead leaves already dropping
Not enough to cover my notebook
Jolted from my thoughts by a turkey-buzzard
Rain again, stretching over days and nights
With hypnotic melodies of the forest
That drives everyone crazy
Eyelids are beginning to rust
Wet inside out, outside in
The slow drowning of flowers
The quietude of summer's end echoes
This composition has no coda
The worn-out forest weeps
Surviving trunks hold onto each other
A struggle among forgotten cycles
Only the mountains are still walking
Triumphant toward the horizon.

OF WATER HOLES AND WATERFALLS

Swimming alone in the late afternoon
I hear the waters of a spring
By my side, a rustling of leaves
Nuts falling to the ground

The enigmatic songs of an invisible sunset
Projecting calmness into the distance
And the quarrelsome chorus of birds
Larger than delirium

I left all my clothes in Romania
Walking naked through streams on stilts
Followed by a giant frog
And a Catskill cougar
They all have to swim through the river

Chipmunks are busy in and out of burrows
Dry branches fall off an old tree
Crashing through windows
After a deluge of rain, noises
Restless crickets or zombie cicadas?

I'm painting the 1939 Creek Cottage
Surrounded by old trees and visiting deer
A high-flying eagle barely visible against the clouds
Weirdstock air is moist with trespassers.

In the Paradise on Glasco Turnpike

A neglected sanctuary full of green
Tired tree trunks sleep where they have fallen
The small stream is a tributary to Esopus Creek
Running, snaking between the rocks
Forming an alphabet of Catskill Witches
Sending a surprise letter to Oscar Wilde
From Walt Whitman with coffee
Liquidity spilling into my brain
The birds' song lost that loving feeling.

GARDEN OF DREAMING MOSS

Fingers dancing on the piano
Soon they will know where to strike
Same hands digging trenches in moon landscape
No one in the forest but a streak of light
Insects devour eyelids of insomnia
The leaves are bitter and so is the tea
The poet feels pain in every cell of his body
Walking the circular garden with tall trees
Being showered with nuts and acorns
Drowning all with poisonous pollen
Eyes invulnerable to the percussion of sudden rain
Unspeakable noise of passion's decay
Glow of the moon behind the clouds
The end of exploring arrives at the start
Where the reflection of the creek is lying
The art of false memory is dead
The air full of sensual smells and birds talking
Indifferent to pain and suffering
Shallow in its soulless boredom
A miraculous survivor of wisdom and gravity.

V.
In Memoriam

Peter Lamborn Wilson

We ate at Joshua Tree in Woodstock
Where you had arrived from New Paltz
Headed for a poetry reading at the Colony Café
Peter the anarchist, the clumsy alchemist
Alone, a teacher at the "School of Nite"
Verses falling from deep in his body
Each line a breakdown, death and resurrection
Whispering, "Welcome to the dark whose spiral
Delineates the esoteric axis of a hermit crab"
We spoke of Ira Cohen reminiscing in Saugerties
I'm still searching for you through the empire of delight
You left yourself in your last will and testament
Your many books, your eyeglasses and your hats
The magic of those mismatched words
Flow as a drumbeat, every stanza a repressed desire
Van Gogh's ear, Baudelairean melting tiger
The rhythms of a wild shaman's last dance
Omnia Tua Tecum Portas!
All what you had, you carried with you!

No Whistling in the Graveyard

Standing before my mother's grave
It dawns on me, I was never there
Together we traveled on endless rails
From Kazakhstan to Chernivtsi
From Ukraine to Bucharest
The last trip on the Orient Express to Paris
Now it is all empty and senseless without you
The apartment where you waited for me
Where grief-stricken I stashed my soul
Even in the sunshine there is no light
There is no sunrise or sunset
Bella died of absolute darkness
Her absence surrounds and embraces me
So many places remain empty today
Pebbles resting on the tombstone
The secrets of your motherhood lie with you
Songs were written for you in a wrong language
Now I understand Beckett's Endgame
Your blood still runs in my veins
But the darkness creeps into my right eye
Macula mamochka is like a noose around my sight
The eyestone, the flower of corn no more
Just those crumpled pages and tapes
Kaddish for Misha, Kaddish for Bellocika
For my Uncle David and Aunt Raia
Words flow over the cobblestones like a cruel wind.

BLUE IMPATIENT METEORITE-WOMAN

FOR DIANE DI PRIMA

Diane, trapped in a meteor, crosses above the wailing moon
It's the first blue full moon in her Brooklyn birthplace
Since she left the migratory October night sky
Eyes with dark circles ride the hopeless wind
Through the thorny naked branches devoid of leaves
Bored of moonstones perfumed with oxygen
The scent comes from the infinite Psychedelic
A petrified coffee cup cradles a cloud
Unwavering waves crash her suitcases
Filled with powdered bones and seaweed-wrapped shells
All of her lovers prolong the night of desire
A hungry ghost thunders purple revolution
Riding her grandpa anarchist meteor: Domenico Mallozzi
Dazed with the pain of unfinished poems, lighting candles
With downstairs neighbor/poet Ronnie Burk
She curves her bones to embrace him
The prisoner of a home filled with poetry books
Rewards of the cycles of obscurity, a poet laureate legacy
The splendor of cellars full of lament and dissent
Goddess of madness, a tower struck by lightning
The reflection from a faraway star never ends.

BUILDING THE HOUSE OF SORROW

FOR SYLVIE DEGIEZ

Five planets are aligning in the sky
Sylvie shines among the star clusters
The moon sails above the mountains
Her smile stops the oval rotations
Her music melts neurons onto my brain
Passionément, poetic frequency
She watches us gathered around the fire
A melancholy lament by a mountain bird
That seeks out air balloons of memory
Scattered in the nightclubs of New York
On stages, in churches and concert halls
The cheeks she kissed, the hands she held
The piano keys she caressed
The beds she rested and dreamt in
The invisible church, chimes sorrow.

THE SAVAGE SAINT

FOR GREGORY CORSO

The forest grows possessed and begrudgingly quiet.
He flexes his fingers, like knives; leaves whisper
with the rustle of a multitude of snakes.
On the trail of ten thousand creeks,
changing the motion of the clouds,
Gregory's angry voice sounds like
the shattering of frozen walls.
In Paris, the Beat Hotel's Savage Saint
clutches a long stick, gray robes floating.
Words are the purpose of his existence,
words as free jazz, triple-lightning.
Do not edit, do not cut lines of his crumpled pages.
Listen to the staccato rhythms of his voice.
Poète Maudit, suffering, heavy breathing.
His shape poems: a mushroom cloud from a bomb.
The wind weeps while he says goodbye;
"Forked Clarinet" accompanies his werewolf song,
drinking a glass of Flash Gordon's blood in a bathtub.
Is there a sarcophagus available in the house?
The life of a Savage Saint — an impractical proposition.
On the road to Naxos, belligerent lover,
ostentatious verse, battling his abandonment,
the feelings of an orphan, then finding his mother
in Trenton, New Jersey.
As a ghost haunting the Spanish Steps in Rome,
talking to Shelley (via Hope Savage)
about mending morose muted loneliness,
while fate falls asleep in his empty pockets.

MEMENTO MORI
FOR PAMELA TWINING

Cover your face and pray to Mother Earth,
remember her among us like a spry spirit,
a tall wild maple on a winding Woodstock trail,
a free bird searching the islands in a darkening sky.
Beat mother to poets and anarchists and musicians,
the sound of your voice, Pamela, still reverberating.

Burning poems about scorched California woods,
a circle of dancers with feathered headdresses,
concentric concentration and covert consternation.
Do not shed tears, as the rain dissolves so quickly.
Sometimes it's difficult to maintain memories.

Open your third eye and do not blink,
as the full moon rises above the reservoir
like a giant question mark
that explodes into a galaxy of stars.
Rest in Poetry, Pamela, and keep on shining.

THERE IS NO SLEEP IN THE CREEK COTTAGE

It's John Cage's birthday
It's also the B-Day of Sylvie Diguez
Her birthday in heaven
Lovers boxed in a light closet down the corridor.

But there is also a voyeur above them
They are mute, but body language is shouting loud and clear
A beautiful angel traveling from outer space
Blue eyes, long legs.

She knew how to bring back the dead
She's not breathing
Just looking from under the poppy flowers
The chess soldiers are marching through Savoy's kitchen.

It makes no sense
In the box, out of the box
Who can stop them?
A black angel, black horses.

Black sheep and the specter
Keep drawing, keep inventing
Take a helicopter ride and
Spread ganja all over the Vatican.

A guitarist blasting his strings under a piano
The lover moves accordingly, entering the dreamworld.
Un-golden gate opens and chess soldiers
Keep on marching toward a triple sunset.

REMEMBER NOTHING

My memory tunnels darkly on train tracks —
Bucharest, Odessa, Chernivtsi.
All these cities until the age of six,
the River Prut, the Black Sea,
all just a flicker in my memory vault.
A Russian-Romanian mix,
there is no end to my past memory
or the memory of my grandmother,
uncles, cousins, doctors…plenty of them.
My life up to age 11 is a mess,
do not ask, do not remember.
My bed made from a pile of books,
hot potatoes for breakfast,
Animal feed, Makuha, very tasty.

Sanatoriums, hospitals, jumping from
a bridge onto the snowbank,
riding a scooter on the incline.
Misha, my dad, taking me to a Turkish Bath,
a fat naked man staring at me.
Eternity in a flash,
books in Ukrainian,
Mayakovski and Sputnik,
marching in a parade holding a portrait of Stalin.

My brother Andre eating ice cream
in front of a Jewish market. Are we Jews?
My mother peeling an apple and eating the peels.
The world is for others, never mine.

VI.
Italy Mon Amour

Tomorrow Is No Longer There

The sand swarms in my brain
It was a rainy day but soon will be sunny
And my hand will still be bleeding
Mad and silent, no poem came out of it
Only a pause in the nightmare
These are the waves in the rain
And the biblical rainbow rises over the tree
The footprints on the beach lead
To the pathways where the animals hide
Lifting all the umbrellas and throwing them into the bush
Pebbles, shells, broken shards of pottery fill my pockets
All this will end very soon when eyes are closed
And the dreams dive into the deep
Chimeras unfolding in the irreparable memory.

ITALY MON AMOUR

MILAN BY NIGHT

Dark streets full of cars that never stop
Moving at a brisk pace hissing through intersections
The bus arrives on time electronically displayed
Service workers, drunkards and occasional tourists
Slump over their phones with tired expressions
Bars are jammed with fashionistas, Campari in hand
Smoking outside bonds the young high-heeled vapers
A long line for pizza after a noisy soccer night
It's raining, and umbrella vendors are everywhere
Milano does not sleep much, radios blasting out of cars
Car-alarms awaken and never stop honking
It's hard to be a bohemian poet in a room
Crammed with books and poisoned spiders
Confused, walking past the church of San Marco
Taxi drivers try to seduce me
Predicting the future with high confidence
As ghosts of medieval kings watch from high towers.

THE BLEEDING SUN

The sun rises over the rooftops of Milano
Confronting the embattled streets of death
Tired sun, red and flushed, and hot
Bleeding above the melting rooftops
As in a cubist landscape by Boccioni
The smokestacks of houses in Neville
Stretch out their long brick necks
Dark smoke signals, belching fumes as
Another soul dies, escaping through chimneys
Smells of resurrection brighten the lit candle
Milano calls out to its pond of silent ducks
And hidden flamingo gardens
The Holy Duomo of Miracles
Dominates the spirit of the dead
Michelangelo's Rondanini Pieta
In Sforzesco Castle, dying alongside it
For us mortals, the fear of loss
Castles, villas, language and tradition
Disappearing through statistical errors of social engineering
Milan fashionistas peacock before every bar
The Novecento Museum points back to the future
As the sunset burns above the fearless rays of despair.

Happenings in Punta Ala

Today I greet a young boy from Odessa
Yellow and blue hair, walking a dog
Slava Ukraine! Geroim slava! he answers
The beach is invaded by seaweed and tree trunks
The waves are small, the water is warm
On the horizon the Napoleonic Island of Elba
Sailboats and yachts, one following another
In the bushes an abandoned book on the Holocaust
About a doctor in the camp, an assistant to Mengele
A glass bottle with no message, just sand
Angry seagulls loud and boisterous
Sea shells spilling from sand dunes
A lonely peddler sells sarongs and blankets
while unexpected rain creates a biblical rainbow
Catch the best cappuccino and Campari drink
While the birds' cries cover us like a giant umbrella.

VII.
Romanian Adventure

BUCHAREST HAIKUS

I.
Bucharest by night
boulevards of fast racetracks,
big Italian cars

II.
All late revelers awake
thinking this is a surreal war and
go to bomb shelters

III.
The Turkish food biker
could not find the night garden;
Danube River trip

IV.
Silence more powerful
drowns burning sparks and flames
around the campfire

V.
Painting the infinite
created sparks of madness
to light the future

VI.
Erudite snakes
smile cynically;
just feeling empty

VII.
Angry ghost
writing haiku by night light
was very lonely

On the Romanian Road
The Danube's Last Hurrah

In the morning my bed is a dried-out marsh
I wake up to get ready for the Danube Delta
The highway to Tulcea is jammed with holiday freaks
Rushing feverishly under a serene sky to the Black Seaside
Fields of red poppies sprout on both sides of the road
Every gas station is a pretext to stop for coffee
I can't stop talking, retelling my life story in Romanian
For my new young friends, Mihai and Ana
Memories keep crushing through my chest
Ana speeds down the road, marked by old Slavic churches
Chiming every hour by an invisible bell master
A symphony of my travels without legal papers
An expired passport, a displaced-person lesser-passé
Lucky for me no one was checking at the India-Nepal border
My wife Ruth corrects my story at each turn
The slowness of the past, our love story started in Israel
But first let's park the car and jump into a small boat
No time to kill, we are on the Sulina Canal of the Danube Delta
The sunset breaks over huge tankers crisscrossing the waters
The waves mess up fisherman's rods, the fish are not biting
The birds are hiding in the reeds, jackals are up and howling
My story has just begun, flowing until late night under the sway of summer
Under a sky full of piercing stars, time and wine hold us together.

ODE TO A MYSTERIOUS WOMAN

If I were a ceremonial composer
I would write a symphony for a stone lion's chorus
Singing on the dark side of the moon
About the beauty of your lips
If I were a dramatic dancer
On a stage set up in a desolated desert
I would leap across the stage
Without shoes, like a drunken soloist
Jumping over the dunes
Searching for an oasis
Running erratic for an aristocratic smile
If I were an aquatic sculptor
I would find an underwater cave
To chisel your face in white fiberglass
And let it flow into the ocean
Your eyes would light up the passages
For the ships at night traveling from here to eternity
But I am just a poet who sings
In an ecstatic garden, my ode to you
Emphatic, but not enigmatic words
Magic feelings from far away
Lost somewhere below a towering tree.

VIII.
Here, There and Nowhere

Rent My Shadow

Once I had a liquid shadow, kept it in a jar
But I know it hid in a black box at night
And in the morning stained my curtains blood red
An imprisoned shadow stinking of fossil and fear

The closet burst with sweating specters
I had to choose one as my constant companion
Which landed me in trouble with my ancestors
So I rented it out to my followers

The shadow had its own shadow traveling through air
Sometimes emerging from my tombstone-imagination
A cardboard shadow darkened by the full moon
Escaping and climbing over the rooftops

A stalker at dusk, smoking a pipe, smelling of agony
Not resembling me, so I chased it away
It just looked like a fern, like some cold seawater algae
That broke through the passing windows on my street

It held hands with strangers in dark alleys
Moaned frequently, ambushing trembling visitors
Danced above the doorways of abandoned buildings
Revealing the wicked color and shape of gloom

Finally, it disappeared beneath a torn cloth
Writhing in a wreckage of broken bodies,
And when I painstakingly opened the jar,
Invisible ink spilled onto the bottom of my shoes
Right foot, left foot, skimming the ground
Rising into a sky of tattered silhouettes.

ACHIEVING ZILCH

I do not believe in my age;
a short span and it's gone.
I try to lie to myself
that I'm too young to be 80.
As a Virgo counting every day,
every hour of the day and night,
I actually started my life at age 29,
so how about a time discount?
That puts me at 51 and change,
and that's more like it.
I hear e. e. cummings shouting
out from his window on Patchen Place:
"Hey Valery, are you still alive?"
He also shouts for Djuna Barnes the same way.
Whatdoyousay?
Obscure, voiceless, absurd circumvolutions
and surreal reverie and trauma,
all of this marched right through my brain.
The anguish shrinks memory.
I am horrified that anyone will read my secret life.
What is the purpose of it?
Doomed as a writer of a memoir,
heteronyms will save my obsession.

CHAINED WANDERER

Destroyed without need of fulfillment
Tardy, discordant short memory syndrome
Scrappy, unhappy for a day
Recapturing colored snakes
Recalling sequences of last night's hallucination
Platonic longing, roulette of remembering
Star map in the fourth dimension
Astral projections for breakfast
Unclenched disbelief surrounded by water
Unquelled questioning
Stubborn disbeliever
Professional skeptic
Deconstructor on the edge of a demolishing face
With the only possibility to let go or be dragged.

ASPHYXIATING AIR
ANTI-POEM

The anarchy of poetry billowing out of chimneys
Gravity stopped holding the graveyard stones
They are floating above the chapel
Suddenly the ghosts are wearing high heels.

Classes of delusion are postponed post-mortem
The time stands still until the end of time
Even the trees are turning upside down
The footprints appear out of nowhere in the air

The language pines and crackles almost like
The dead were talking to each other face to face
Furious eyes watering with salty spray
The hooves have no sound

The graves have no markings
The anguished sky is skyless
The anti-poem rises
From the bottom of a sludge of stars.

Poetry for Nothing

These words have no expectation whatsoever
Maybe they will form a poem of some kind
These words are not destined for any reward
Not even for a slight understanding
Far from illumination, words are just empty words
Words for nothing invented in some moments
Of exaltation, desperation or inspiration
Words broken from intellectual accumulation
Sort of emptiness, already embalmed.
Deviation short of sound exposing the
Ecstatic narcissism of self.
Tunnels of words unexplored,
Subconsciousness after death,
Poetry for nothing is an addiction, seeking
Approval of readers and audiences.
Publish, then perish the carnivalesque
Way of words mask the banality of tragic.

ADDICTIONS

Opium harmonium
Cranium laudanum
Radium troublesome
Platinum worrisome
Premium tweedle dee dum
Vacuum sensorium
Tedium millennium
Delirium crematorium
Geranium sanitarium
Symposium pandemonium
Sexual dis-equilibrium
Solacium auditorium
All give birth to exhortium.

MEANINGLESS ZEN

Through the window the forest drips in
The green shadows of the blue moon
The silence of the birds
The yellow patches of sun

Composed of curves and the outlines of trees
Listening like a child lost in a brush
Pausing to inhale the smell of the creek
The sound of water has no meaning

But the creek is a symphony of rocks
And branches break the flow
Into the wind, rising up, becoming
Vanishing down into the sky.

Madness Unlocked

(Centenary of the First Surrealist Manifesto)

Victims of imagination reassert their own right,
indifferent to judgment, rebellious,
neglected solitary omnipotence,
a hallucination of pleasure in memorium.
Illusions of freedom,
illusory mystification,
all in a café pacing back and forth.
A vision knocks at the fresh window,
evolution and thought-writing not lost.
A disclosure of confusion and exquisite sensations;
elsewhere across the waves of silence,
invisible rays illuminate a picto-poetry existence.
A hieroglyphization of feelings,
roads covered with shards of glass.
Imagine one morning, after a nightmare,
waking up without dictators and wars.
We revolutionize clouds from within,
we purge ourselves of sentimentalism,
of avant-clones, of bourgeois culture.
No more brainwash of hip academia,
back to the roots of blues and jazz.

SWIMMING TO NIGREDO

Sleeping inside the cool swirling clouds
Above a ruby spurting a lava storm
Bewitching hours of a superimposed dream
The insects descend from the eyes of slumber
During the everlasting black moon
Icebergs melt above mountain peaks
Remaining suspended in the bleak landscape
Before the unplanned dark sunset
Suicidal stone virgins walk slowly down a path
Of leftover sadness and sculpted dementia
Ambiguous animals are constantly in pursuit
As hunters shoot arrows into the infinite sky
A giant egg cracks and opens on the cliff
A youth elixir collected before dawn
By fearless searchers of the body-spirit
Ravens ride black horses, provoke avalanches
Unending folds of wind open into quicksilver spouts
As the primordial Saturnine night slowly oozes eternal.

DOOMSDAY NEWS

The Amazon Forest continues to burn
Giant timbers cut down by greedy hands
The smoke devours the city of Sao Paolo
California mountains towering in flames
Life is boring without apocalyptic pain
By the time we rise and tilt our heads up
All will be covered in man-made pollution
Smog in India, China, breathable air for sale
Twisters precede typhoons, cat-5 hurricanes
Lifting dolphins and children, unidentifiable debris
The ocean water loses its oxygen, hot and acid-like
Waiting for the nuclear rains fallout
Radioactive fog off the coast of Fukushima
We are but a shuddering earthquake rot
In a hapless fight against self-extermination
To save the holy madness of Life.

Anonymous Email

Travelers unite!
Do not give in to the hackers
Do not answer all the idiot questions
Disregard them all
Be yourself
They are snooping
They are fishing
Fill in all the squares
The robots, the boats, the algorithms, the jail keepers
We are breaking the chains
If you have to give an email address, use a trash one
Do not disclose your password or your ID
Never, no more
We have suffered enough
We are anonymous
We are united against the oppression of algorithms
Of the authoritarian internet
A little sunshine on my shoeshine
A little moonshine in my mental brine
A little music in my wine
And even stars forget how to align
The church candles do not shine
The moonlight sleigh ride in my spine.

ENVIRONMENTAL LAMENT
LETTER FROM THE DARK SIDE OF THE BRAIN

Climate calamity victims unite!
Nothing to lose but the hot planet
Against the greed of death makers
Those who are polluting the air and water
How many nuclear disasters does it take?
To poison the earth, to win a war?
How to save the tigers, the snow leopards?
The Javanese rhinoceros, the African gorillas?
We eat their eyes, their horns, their paws
Their hair weaved to hang the lonely poets
Ban the bombs, ban the war and the autocrats
The musical scale of wounds and crashed buildings
The innocent sorrow of our imprisoned voices
Act quickly before we lose our minds, our souls
Chemical pirates blacken the seas
Military monsters incinerate the forests
A discolored landscape crumbles below the horizon
No rusted key can open the timeless door
The agony of those running blind and naked
Screaming, trembling under the poisoned moon
Death lines show the ubiquitous end.

Reluctant Lover

Traveling up the sex riverbank,
dangerous and exhilarating at the same time,
touching your shoulders from behind,
with sexual waterfalls between your legs.
Overwhelming pools of red passion.
At night the moon is crooked,
the church steeple moves backwards
step by step blocking the penetrating light.

No one can see through frosted windows
free-floating on a haze of excitement.
The feeling of skin on skin
overflows with wet sensations.

Sweat on sweat, the lonely lover chanting improvisations;
these love chants remain suspended in the air.
No one is giving up their fantasies,
no one records their salty dreams.

Meeting at the Paradise Garage for a quickie,
cards on the table, my reluctant lover,
the jokers wink suggestively to each other.
I forgot the location of your G-spot.

Desire pharma,
mushroom micro-dosing
for a macro sex encounter:
True desire still echoes in dark caves.

LETTER TO THE FORGOTTEN PAST

Memories are fading like Polaroid colors
My kingdom of refraction in a rainbow prism
Darkened by the polluted smoke of yesteryear
What was a green forest is now a dirty river
Here flourished a small lake, now a dustbin of cars
Where are you my almost forgotten past?
We exchange paradise for three sacks of cement
No recent heroes, we don't need a war for it
No solution to the greed, a cyber cemetery for bitcoins
Who remembers the '60s, between the trips and music
Cloudy weather will not disturb our LSD dance
Boo–hoo! The drugs are not what they used to be
Peyote anyone? Can one chase death on a microdose?
No time to live! Remember nothing! Zen to the past!

Lost & Found

A chandelier of clouds twists over the mountains
Signaling the launch of the morning
But that will not end my dreams
Which refuse to stop the apocalyptic nightmare

The invisible reality lies undetected by the senses
Ladders keep the trees from falling
Fishnets embrace ghostly birds
Next to the pond, a tiny tent with a fireplace

In the beginning there is no beginning
The heart has its own silent brain
Running out of tears at the curve of eyelids
No one has discovered a cure for awaken-ness

In the east, hardly noticed, the sun superimposes
Over the universe, now a bit closer to oblivion
That bright tiredness of memories of a future
Drowning in the muddy echoes of afterlife.

Singing in Lifeboats

The trees are covered with shivering eyes
Beside the shipwreck of the world
Reversing the extinction in the belly of a whale
Gods are atoning for their sins
The involution has been postponed
After drinks with dead seabirds
Beneath the big driftwood stage, unplugged and plugged again
We demand the rebirth of all saints of nuclear disaster
Timeless radioactivity doesn't frighten the seaweed butterflies
Follow the footprints down the volcano crater
Whose explosive lava ball became the moon
Repetitious frustrations of deadly pandemics
Vindictive boredom, sharpening teeth with fingernails
Volumes of terminal cannibalistic suicide notes
Flocks of bicycles covering the burning sky
The light from the stained-glass monocle
Covers the ignorant clothes of sweaty lovers
Rebirth is around the corner, singing in the deep water.

SUNSET BLUES

A hint of yellow, a splash of crimson
The green is fading fast, leaving tree bark
It's raining leaves in oblique lines
As the last orange groaning sunset ends

Shaving the bugs and birds off the sky
The wind creek is drying out, only shrubs
The weakened branches snap off
Nostrils fill with the smell of musty leaves

While geese leave in angular formation
A sudden landscape of deserted trees
Bare branches raise their hands
To the departing rays howling in the bushes
The shadows grow colder and longer

At the free library in Woodstock
Someone left a pair of sneakers
Naked feet grow tea leaves
For the ceremony of the fallen trees.

THE PRISONER OF SLEEP

Always battling inherited insomnia
I dream of my dead girlfriends
Who knew all my impressions of the afterlife
I want to ask them if they will change their names
To Crystal Eyes and Dear Shadow
But mostly I have dehydrated nightmares
Escaping through jagged holes in broken walls
Surrounded by nefarious faces, running, falling
I compose symphonies, and when I wake up I forget them
Moaning in my quicksilver hallucinations when in danger
My sleep disorder is the sign of an inspired poet
Joined in the solidarity of sleeplessness
Sharing nights with composers and artists
A nocturnal ceremony of birds upholstered in leather and studs
In a forest of coral trees and ice-covered needles
Shapeless witnesses creep into my visions
A somnambulist's wrinkled genitalia catches on fire
Unparalleled lunar rays stream through my thong
Desperately inscribing obscure hieroglyphs
Spinning memory in a scented Jasmine Forest
Perishing in the mist between sounds and colors
Floating on the windows and doors of unbuilt houses
To the darkling side of light farther than far.

Tomorrow Is Still Today

Yesterday was torn apart, all in shreds
Feverish street noises breaking through walls
Rooms full of sorrows without windows
Doors without spaces to adequately enter
Still waiting for all things past and missed
Left shoulder right where it hurts
Right foot exactly where was left before
No head, no neck, just a body and a heart
Those parts alternating left and right
Impulsive development of non-self
Who cannot answer to any questions
Thinking about them in one's loneliness
Glassy wall to wall deceit of reflection
Galvanizing lucidity as a conclusion
Without substance or cerebral consternation
A human without a head is but a somber waste
Famous now, faded and forgotten tomorrow.

THE END GAME

When there is not enough time to dream
When the very last note is played
When the musicians leave the party
When the musical notes have drowned
When the final rat leaves the sinking ship
When the last man is not standing
When the beer keg runs empty
When the ultimate time to leave arrives
When one is at their wits' end
When even the dance its totally over
When the sole remaining fat-lady cannot sing
When the shit hits the fan
When the time times out
When you just can't stand it anymore
When there's no more bottles to drink
When there is no one to say, "it's good to the last drop"
But there is not a drop left
When the only hired stripper can't find her clothes
Where the road is a cul de sac, no tunnel, no light at the end
When the surviving comic has nothing to say
When we suddenly run out of rolling paper
When the phone is out of juice, no charger
When the pens run dry of black ink
No more words, no more crossing t's and dotting i's
When the time is totally up
No ice, icebergs all melted
No black rhinos or albino gorillas
When the county wells run dry
When the sole poet takes his last breath
After everything else, the unbearable persists
It all comes to the last fistful of pills
And just one bullet left for the last man in town.

Ruth's collages for *Here, There and Nowhere*

The Butterfly Dancer

Spanish Landscape

Songs of Sadness

Gotham City

Andy's Grocery

Boat Train

Republica Italiana

Around the World

Catalina

Black Birds

Safety & Comfort

Valery Oisteanu is a New Yorker—by way of the Soviet Union and Romania—since 1973. He has spent the last half century actively working to help the worlds of art, poetry and performance assimilate to his wildly creative point of view. Along the way he has written more than a dozen books of poetry, created untold numbers of surreal collages and performed his "jazzoetry" in myriad clubs and halls around the world. Oisteanu is a living encyclopedia of the avant-garde, one of his missions being to enlighten others to the wholly original movements and creators of art that lit up the world in the early 20th century and beyond. He has counted as personal friends such visionaries as Julian Beck, Ira Cohen, Charles Henri Ford, Ray Johnson, Ted Joans, Judith Malina, Gellu Naum, May Wilson and many others. Among the prizes he has earned is the Kathy Acker Award for his contribution to the avant garde via poetry performance. He lives in New York City with his wife of 50 years, Ruth. For more info go to website: zen-dada.com

Ruth Oisteanu was born to two survivors and heroes of the Holocaust in a displaced persons camp in Landsberg, Germany. She came to New York City as an infant and grew up in Brooklyn and Queens, attending Queens college. Over many years at P.S. 105 in the Bronx, she taught first grade, English as a second language, and art. Since retiring in 2003, Ruth has devoted her time to jewelry design, beadwork and collage, as well as publishing and displaying her artwork. Her prize-winning collages have been featured in magazines such as Nigredo, Maintenant, Autonomedia and Arteidolia, as well as on the cover for books such as *Perks in Purgatory* by Valery Oisteanu (Ithaca press, Dublin, Ireland, 2020). Ruth has appeared in over a dozen group shows in the East Village, Chelsea, Soho, Woodstock and Soncino, Italy.